Looking for Treasure

Contents

Written and photographed by Lara Maiklem

Collins

Looking for treasure

Our world is full of treasures that have been lost and forgotten, but you need to search to find them.

Kit list

- boots
- bag or **knapsack**
- magnifying glass
- small **trowel**

3

Beaches

A strange collection of things wash up on beaches. Sometimes they have been floating offshore for years and have travelled many miles.

Remember!
Take only pictures and leave only footprints.

The strandline

When the tide goes out, it leaves
a strandline on the shore where you can
comb for treasures the sea leaves behind.

seaweed

crab shell

mermaid's purse (the egg case of a shark)

Pebbles

Look for unusual pebbles.
Take a picture to remind you of a day
out on the seashore.

pebble with
a hole

Shells

You might find empty shells washed up on the strandline. See how many different sorts you can find.

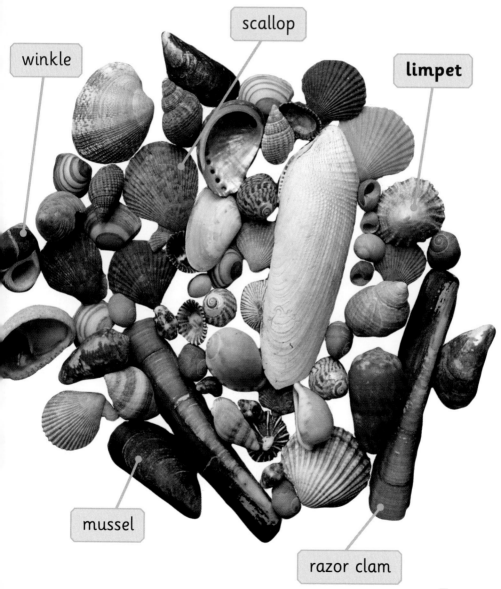

scallop

winkle

limpet

mussel

razor clam

Sea glass

It can take decades for the sea to turn broken glass into precious sea treasure.

red is rare

green is common

Fossils

Fossils are the remains of ancient creatures and plants that have turned into special stones.

sea urchin

ammonite

large shark tooth

crinoids

Rivers

Rivers can hide strange possessions and things that were thrown away.

Remember!
Only explore riverbanks with an adult.

Mudlarks

A mudlark searches for objects on river **foreshores**.
Here I am, I am a mudlark!

Rubbish

Throughout history, people have flung unwanted possessions into rivers. Sadly, most modern rubbish is plastic.

Pottery

The edges of rivers are a great place to find ancient broken pottery, called shards.

potter's thumb mark

broken teacup

Bottles

Old bottles sometimes emerge from riverbanks. They are made from glass and pottery, and come in unusual shapes.

pottery lemonade bottle

blue glass

Coins

People throw coins into rivers for luck. This superstition has been around for hundreds of years.

large old penny

ancient Roman coin

precious silver coin

Fields

Fields are a great place to look for treasure.

Remember!
Always get permission from the owner of the land first.

Animal excavations

Animals sometimes excavate things when they are burrowing.

coin

molehill

ancient pottery

Stone tools

Many years ago, people made stone tools by **knapping** them with great precision. They were lost or thrown away when they were damaged.

spearhead

arrowhead

sharp cutting blade

Feathers

Found bird feathers can make a special collection.
Here are eight feathers.

buzzard feather

pigeon feather

grey feather

large seagull feather

House

If you live in an old house, a progression of people will have lived there before. Look for treasures they left behind.

Gardens

Treasures sometimes emerge when you are gardening.

Tiny things

Peer into cracks and under floorboards for tiny possessions that were once lost.

pins

thimble

beads

jewel

Toys

Look for toys that were mislaid by children years ago.

metal toy

marble

Glossary

ammonite a fossilised sea creature
buzzard large bird of prey
crinoids fossilised sea creatures
foreshore the part of the riverbank that can get
   covered by water when the tide comes in
knapping chipping and flaking stone to make tools
knapsack backpack
limpet a sea snail that lives on rocks
trowel a small digging tool

Index

Vale of York hoard

This amazing hoard of Viking treasure was found by a father and son in 2007.

Viking bracelets

silver cup

Make a time capsule

Hide a time capsule for the future.
Include possessions that will
give information about how we
live today.

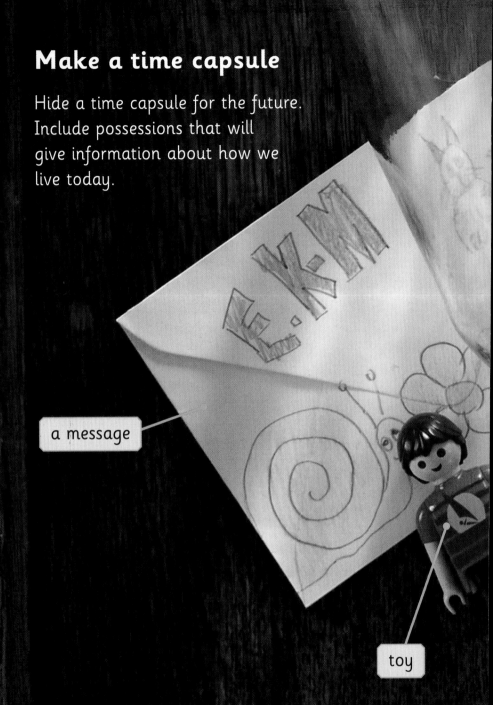

a message

toy

art gallery in the UK and is
kside Power Station in
was in use from 1893
Modern in 2000.

A solar farm.

Solar farm powers hospital

A solar farm in Wales has, at times, provided all the energy needed to run Morriston Hospital in Swansea. A solar farm is a large collection of solar panels that collect energy from the Sun and turn it into electricity. It was hoped that the solar farm would provide a fifth of the hospital's energy every year. However, this target has already been beaten and the hospital has saved £120,000 in electricity bills since the nearby farm opened in November.

newspaper clipping

Treasure hunt

Pick some objects from this treasure and decide where they might have come from.

Review: After reading

Use your assessment from hearing the children read to choose any GPCs, words or tricky words that need additional practice.

Read 1: Decoding

- Encourage the children to work out the meaning of these words (which have more than one meaning) in context:
  page 5 **comb** (*search carefully*)   page 8 **common** (*found in large numbers*)
  page 20 **progression** (*series, number of*)

- To help the children read longer words, encourage them to sound and blend each "chunk" or syllable:
  trea/sures   coll/ec/tion   preci/ous   poss/essi/ons   anci/ent
  o   Can the children identify how /sh/ or /zh/ are written in these words?

- Point to labels and encourage fluency by asking: Can you blend these words silently in your head as you read these words aloud?

Read 2: Prosody

- Discuss how the children would read page 4 if they were a broadcaster on a television programme. Ask: Which words would you emphasise to get the viewers' attention? (e.g. *strange, years, many*)

- Challenge the children to read page 5, reminding them to keep an enthusiastic tone and to think about which words they might emphasise. (e.g. *strandline, comb, treasure*)

Read 3: Comprehension

- Give the children the following statements. For each statement ask: Is this true or false? Which clues helped you decide?
  o   There are very few places where you can find treasure. (*false: e.g. you can find them in rivers, shores, fields, gardens*)
  o   It's not easy to find treasures on the strandline. (*true: you have to "comb", page 5*)
  o   You can always find treasure in modern rubbish. (*false: "most modern rubbish is plastic", page 12*)

- Look together at pages 30 and 31. Where do the children think the treasures might have been found? Do they recognise any from earlier in the book?

- Bonus content: Read pages 28 and 29 aloud to the children. Discuss what information the objects give "about how we live today". Ask the children what information the treasures on pages 13, 14, 18, 22 and 23 give about past lives.

🐾 Review: After reading 🐾

Use your assessment from hearing the children read to choose any GPCs, words or tricky words that need additional practice.

Read 1: Decoding

- Encourage the children to work out the meaning of these words (which have more than one meaning) in context:
  page 5 **comb** (*search carefully*)   page 8 **common** (*found in large numbers*) page 20 **progression** (*series, number of*)
- To help the children read longer words, encourage them to sound and blend each "chunk" or syllable:
  trea/sures   coll/ec/tion   preci/ous   poss/essi/ons   anci/ent
  o   Can the children identify how /sh/ or /zh/ are written in these words?
- Point to labels and encourage fluency by asking: Can you blend these words silently in your head as you read these words aloud?

Read 2: Prosody

- Discuss how the children would read page 4 if they were a broadcaster on a television programme. Ask: Which words would you emphasise to get the viewers' attention? (e.g. *strange, years, many*)
- Challenge the children to read page 5, reminding them to keep an enthusiastic tone and to think about which words they might emphasise. (e.g. *strandline, comb, treasure*)

Read 3: Comprehension

- Give the children the following statements. For each statement ask: Is this true or false? Which clues helped you decide?
  o   There are very few places where you can find treasure. (*false: e.g. you can find them in rivers, shores, fields, gardens*)
  o   It's not easy to find treasures on the strandline. (*true: you have to "comb", page 5*)
  o   You can always find treasure in modern rubbish. (*false: "most modern rubbish is plastic", page 12*)
- Look together at pages 30 and 31. Where do the children think the treasures might have been found? Do they recognise any from earlier in the book?
- Bonus content: Read pages 28 and 29 aloud to the children. Discuss what information the objects give "about how we live today". Ask the children what information the treasures on pages 13, 14, 18, 22 and 23 give about past lives.

31